1 MONTH OF
FREE
READING

at

www.ForgottenBooks.com

By purchasing this book you are eligible for one month membership to ForgottenBooks.com, giving you unlimited access to our entire collection of over 700,000 titles via our web site and mobile apps.

To claim your free month visit:

www.forgottenbooks.com/free225891

ISBN 978-0-266-21653-7
PIBN 10225891

THE STATE HOUSE

IN

BOSTON, MASSACHUSETTS.

BY

DAVID PULSIFER.

" The New State House: may its corner-stone be the '*rights of man*' — its
roof, wisdom; and its walls, patriotism." — JULY 4, 1795.

BOSTON :
RAND, AVERY, AND COMPANY,
PRINTERS TO THE COMMONWEALTH.
1881.

ARMS OF THE COMMONWEALTH OF MASSACHUSETTS.

In Council, Wednesday Dec. 13th, 1780.

Ordered, That Nathan Cushing, Esq., be a Committee to prepare a Seal for the Commonwealth of Massachusetts, who reported a Device for a Seal for said Commonwealth, as follows, viz.: —

Sapphire, an Indian dressed in his Shirt, Moggosins, belted proper, in his right Hand a Bow, *Topaz*, in his left an Arrow, its point towards the Base; of the second, on the Dexter side of the Indian's head, a Star, *Pearl*, for one of the United States of America. Crest, — On a wreath a Dexter Arm clothed and ruffled proper, grasping a Broad Sword, the Pummel & Hilt, *Topaz*, with this Motto — ENSE PETIT PLACIDAM SUR LIBERTATE QUIETEM — and around the Seal — SIGILLUM REIPUBLICÆ MASSACHUSETTENSIS.

Advised that the said Report be accepted as the Arms of the Commonwealth of Massachusetts. — [Council Records, Dec. 13th, 1780.

OFFICES IN THE STATE HOUSE.

WEST WING. — First Floor.
Front.

ADJUTANT-GENERAL.
[Where the military records are carefully kept.]
BOARD OF STATE CHARITIES.

Rear.

SECRETARY OF STATE.
[Here the Records and Archives of the Colony, Province and
Commonwealth are faithfully preserved and kept; the
Records of the Massachusetts Company, commencing in
the year 1628. In this department is the original Charter
granted by Charles the First, A. D. 1628; also, second
Charter, by William and Mary, and Explanatory Charter
by George I.
There is also a Manifesto and Proclamation, on parchment,
of the Commissioners of Great Britain appointed by
George III. for effecting "a reunion and coalition with
her colonies," " with the exemption from any imposition
of taxes by the Parliament." Dated October 3, 1778.]

SECOND FLOOR.
STATE LIBRARY; SECRETARY OF BOARD OF EDUCATION.

THIRD FLOOR.
EXECUTIVE DEPARTMENT.
SPEAKER OF THE HOUSE OF REPRESENTATIVES.

BASEMENT. — [*Entrance on Mount Vernon Street.*]
DOCUMENT ROOM OF THE SECRETARY OF THE COMMONWEALTH.
SECRETARY OF THE BOARD OF AGRICULTURE.
VISITING AGENT OF THE BOARD OF STATE CHARITIES.

EAST WING. — FIRST FLOOR.

Front.

SERGEANT-AT-ARMS.   O. F. MITCHELL.

[This officer, when the General Court is in session, performs
the duties of Sergeant-at-Arms to both branches, has the
general charge and oversight of the State House, and
under his direction every facility is afforded for visiting
the cupola, halls and offices.]

AUDITOR.

Rear.

TREASURER.
DEPUTY TAX COMMISSIONER.
COMMISSIONER OF CORPORATIONS.

SECOND FLOOR.

CLERK OF THE HOUSE OF REPRESENTATIVES.
LEGISLATIVE DOCUMENT ROOM.

THIRD FLOOR.

REPRESENTATIVES' HALL AND SENATE CHAMBER.
PRESIDENT AND CLERK OF THE SENATE.   [*Rear of the Senate
Chamber.*]

BASEMENT. — [*Entrance on Mount Vernon Street.*]

COMMISSIONERS OF PRISONS.
SURGEON-GENERAL.
STATE BOARD OF HEALTH, LUNACY AND CHARITY.
COMMISSIONERS OF SAVINGS BANKS.

DESCRIPTION OF THE STATE HOUSE.

THE land on which the State House stands, formerly belonged to Governor HANCOCK. Its foundation is about 100 feet above the level of the harbor.

It has been said that " the beauty and advantages of this situation, which induced the Legislature to make choice of it for the present building, are acknowledged by both natives and foreigners. It vies with the most picturesque scenes in Europe, and will bear comparison with the castle hill of Edinburgh, the famous bay of Naples, or any other most commanding prospect."

Previous to its enlargement a few years since, it was described as an oblong building, 173 feet front and 61 deep; it consists externally of a basement story, 20 feet high, and a principal story, 30 feet. This, in the centre of the front, is covered with an attic 60 feet wide, 20 feet high, which is covered with a pediment. Immediately above this rises a dome, 50 feet diameter and 30 feet high; the whole terminates with an elegant circular lanthorn. The basement story is finished plain on the wings, with square windows. The centre is 94 feet in length, and formed of arches which project 14 feet; they form a covered walk below, and support a colonnade of Corinthian columns of the same extent above. The outside walls are of large patent bricks. The lower story is divided into a large hall or public walk in the centre, 55 feet square, and 20 feet high, supported by Doric columns; two entries, each 16 feet wide, with two flights of stairs in each; and at the ends offices for the Treasurer, Secretary, Adjutant and Quartermaster General.

The whole cost of the building amounted to $133,333.33. The enlargement cost $243,203.86.

The following account of laying the corner stone is taken from the " Columbian Centinel," of Wednesday, July 8, 1795 : —

MASONIC CELEBRATION.

THE GOVERNOR — being complimented by the Agents of the Commonwealth for building the intended *State House*, with laying the corner stone thereof, His Excellency requested the assistance of the Grand Lodge therein.   Accordingly on *Saturday* last, the Lodges assembled at the Representatives' Chamber, and proceeded in masonic order to the *Old South Meeting-House*, to attend the Oration.   After which the whole proceeded in the following order: —

Independent Fusiliers,
Martial musick
Two Toilers
The CORNER STONE,
[On a truck, decorated with ribbons, drawn by
15 white horses, each with a leader.]
Operative Masons.
Grand Marshal.
Stewards, with staves.
Entered-Apprentices, and Fellow crafts.
Three Master-Masons, bearing the *Square, Level*
and *Plumb-Rule.*
Three Stewards, bearing *Corn, Wine* and *Oil.*
Master Masons.
Officers of Lodges in their respective jewels.
Past-Masters, Royal Arch, &c.
Grand Toiler.
Band of Musick — decorated.
Grand Stewards,
Grand Deacons with Wands,
Grand Treasurer and Grand Secretary,
Past Grand Wardens,
Grand Senior and Junior Wardens,
Past Grand Masters
Rev. Clergy — Brothers —
Grand Master attended by the Deputy-Grand
Master, and Grand Stewards.
Deputy Grand Marshal.
Sheriff of Suffolk.
The Agents of the Commonwealth.
His Excellency THE GOVERNOR,
Honor LT. GOVERNOR,
Adjutant-General, Quarter-Master-General.
Hon. Council,
Members of Legislature —
Clergy, and Strangers of distinction.

In this order, they moved to the spot intended for the edifice; and the procession being opened, the Agents, His Excellency the Governor, the Grand Lodge, Lt. Governor, &c., passed through: and, the operative masons having prepared the Stone, His Excelleney laid it, with the assistance of the Grand and Deputy Grand Master, after having deposited thereunder a silver plate, bearing the following

INSCRIPTION —

This Corner Stone of a Building
intended for the use of the *Legislative*,
and *Executive* branches of GOVERNMENT
of the
Commonwealth of MASSACHUSETTS,
was laid by
His Excellency SAMUEL ADAMS, Esq.,
Governor of said Commonwealth;
Assisted by the Most Worshipful PAUL REVERE,
Grand Master,
And the Right Worshipful WILLIAM SCOLLAY,
Deputy Grand Master,
The Grand Wardens and Brethren
of the
GRAND LODGE of MASSACHUSETTS,
On the FOURTH Day of JULY
AN. DOM. 1795.
A. L. 5795
Being the XXth Anniversary of AMERICAN
INDEPENDENCE.

After which the Governor made the following Address:
" FELLOW CITIZENS,

" The Representatives of the people in General Court assembled, did solemnly Resolve, that an Edifice be erected upon this spot of ground for the purpose of holding the Public Councils of the Commonwealth of Massachusetts. By the request of their Agents and Commissioners, I do now lay the Corner Stone.

" May the Superstructure be raised even to the top Stone without any untoward accident, and remain permanent as the everlasting mountains. May the principles of our excellent Constitution, founded in nature and in the Rights of Man, be ably defended here: And may the same principles be deeply engraven on the hearts of all citizens, and there be fixed unimpaired and in full vigor till time shall be no more."

The whole then returned to the *Council-Chamber*, where the procession broke up.

It is utterly impossible to do justice to the scene which presented itself, on this brilliant occasion.

In 1855, on placing new underpinning under the State House, to correspond with that of the addition or enlargement built that year the workmen unexpectedly found the corner stone in the south-east corner in a damaged condition. The silver plate and coins deposited in 1795, being covered only with a piece of sheet lead, were very much corroded with rust; but after being restored to their original condition, there was then engraved on the reverse side of the silver plate the following inscription : —

The Corner Stone of the Capitol
having been removed in consequence of
alterations and additions to the Building,
The original deposit, together with this
inscription, is replaced by
the Most Worshipful Winslow Lewis, M. D.,
Grand Master,
and other Officers and Brethren of the
Grand Lodge of Massachusetts,
in presence of
His Excellency Henry J. Gardner,
Governor of the Commonwealth,
on the 11 day of August, A. D. 1855.
A. L. 5855.
JOSEPH R. RICHARDS,
SAMUEL K. HUTCHINSON, } *Commissioners.*
GEORGE M. THATCHER,

The plate, with additional coins of 1855, etc., was then deposited, and a new stone was thus laid in the same corner; the condition of that part of the building, resting on shores, not allowing sufficient time for any extended notice or more public ceremonies.

On Wednesday, January 10, 1798, the General Court met in the Old State House, where for about fifty years their sessions had been held, when information was given that the New State House was so far completed that it was in a proper situation to accommodate the Governor and Council, the Senate and House of Representatives.

The next day, January 11, a joint committee waited on His Excellency INCREASE SUMNER, Governor, and the Hon.

crable Council, and requested "them to join the General Court in procession from the Old State House to said new House at 12 o'clock."

The following account and extract from the Speech of Governor Sumner are copied from the " Independent Chronicle " of that date : —

Massachusetts' Legislature.

January 11.

THE two branches of the Legislature having received the report of their committee, agreed to move in procession to the New State House, at 12 o'clock.

A Committee was appointed to wait upon His Excellency the Governor and the Honorable Council, to invite them to the contemplated Procession. At 12 o'clock His Excellency and the Hon. Council, attended the Hon. Legislature, previously convened in the Senate Chamber, and the Procession was formed, consisting of His Excellency the Governor — His Honor the Lieutenant Governor — the Honorable Council — President and Members of the Honorable Senate — Speaker and Members of the Honorable House of Representatives — Secretary of the Commonwealth — State Treasurer — and the respective Secretary's Clerks and Messengers of the different Departments, and proceeded to the future scene of the Public Labors.

When arrived at the New State House they entered the Representatives' Hall, and after a few moments pause — the Presence, Aid and Blessing of the Supreme Law-Giver was invoked by the Rev. Dr. THACHER, in a Prayer peculiarly elegant and pertinent. His Excellency the Governor, His Honor the Lieutenant Governor, and the other Officers of the Government, then withdrew to their appropriate Chambers; and the Hon. House proceeded to business.

His Excellency, by Message acquainted the House, that he would meet them to-morrow at 12 o'clock, for the purpose of addressing them.

FRIDAY JAN. 12.

Agreeable to assignment the two Branches having assembled in the Representatives' Chamber, his Excellency the Governor came in and delivered the following

SPEECH:

Gentlemen of the Senate, and
     Gentlemen of the House of Representatives

WHILE I rejoice with you, and my fellow-citizens at large, on the completion of this stately Edifice, not less honorable to the Commonwealth, at whose expense it was erected, than ornamental to the capital which generously provided the place; permit me to express my entire satisfaction at the ingenious manner in which the plan has been executed. Begun and finished in little more than two years, it exhibits a pleasing proof of the architectural skill and fidelity of your agents, who planned and superintended the work, while it demonstrates the ability of the artificers who performed it.

Combining the advantages of suitable retirement, a healthy situation, and delightful prospect, with such elegant and very convenient apartments, for the security of the Records, and for transacting the public business, there is perhaps no public building to be found within the United States, more useful and magnificent. I am confident that you, Gentlemen of both Houses of the Legislature, will cordially join me in the fervent wish that this State House may long remain a monument of the public spirit of the citizens of Massachusetts, as well as a testimony of their respect to our happy political institutions. We will then, under the smiles of Heaven, unite in dedicating it to the *Honor*, *Freedom*, *Independence* and *Security* of our Country. In this House, may the true principles of the best system of civil government the world has ever seen, be uniformly supported. Here, may every practice and principle be successfully opposed, that tend to impair it. Here, may every act of the Legislature, be the result of cool deliberation and sound judgment. And in this House, on all necessary occasions, may the Supreme Executive, agreeably to the laws of the land, in mercy, cause judgment to be executed. And each branch of our elective government, continuing faithful in the discharge of its trust, God grant, that neither external force or influence, nor internal commotion or violence may ever shake the pillars of our free Republic.

DORIC HALL.

The visitor to the State House, on entering the Doric Hall, will meet with several objects of historic interest: — the statue of Washington, by Sir F. Chantrey, in the rotunda; fac-similes of the Memorial Tablets of the Ancestors of Washington, in front of the statue; two brass cannon formerly belonging to an artillery company in Concord, and two brass cannon captured in the War of 1812; statue of Governor Andrew; busts of President Lincoln, Henry Wilson and Charles Sumner.

Here may be seen the flags of most of the regiments of

the Massachusetts Volunteers, who served during the war of the rebellion, 1861–1865. Deposited here Dec. 21, 1865.

On the eastern wall are four tablets " taken from the base of a Doric column, erected in 1791, by the citizens of Boston on the top of Beacon Hill. The column took the place of an old wooden beacon, blown down November 26th, 1789, which gave its name to the hill and street on which the State House now stands, and stood many feet above the roofs of the houses on the westerly corner of Temple and Mount Vernon Streets, and commanded a view of the harbor and of the environs of the city. It was surmounted by the Gilded Eagle which is now placed over the Speaker's chair in the House of Representatives," and was taken down in 1811 by Mr. Atherton Haugh Stevens, late of East Cambridge, deceased, who made a record, of which the following is a true copy : —

" BOSTON, July 11, 1811.

At 3 o'clock this afternoon, I lowered the Eagle from Beacon Hill Monument.

At the same time on the next day I undermined and dropped from the Hill the monument, and no harm was done to any person.

In the month of June previous I had a dream. I dreamed that I was doing the very same work above stated, not knowing it was to be done.

A. H. STEVENS."

These tablets contain the following inscriptions : —

TO · COMMEMORATE
THAT · TRAIN · OF · EVENTS
WHICH · LED .
TO · THE · AMERICAN · REVOLUTION
AND · FINALLY · SECURED
LIBERTY · AND · INDEPENDENCE
TO · THE · UNITED · STATES
THIS · COLUMN · IS · ERECTED
BY · THE · VOLUNTARY · CONTRIBUTION
OF · THE · CITIZENS
OF · BOSTON

M D C C X C.

Stamp Act passed 1765, repealed 1766.
Board of Customs established 1767.
British troops fired on the inhabitants of Boston
March 5. 1770.
Tea act passed 1773.
Tea destroyed in Boston Decem: 16.
Port of Boston shut and guarded June 1. 1774.
General Congress at Philadelphia Sept: 4.
Provincial Congress at Concord Oct: 11.
Battle of Lexington April 19. 1775.
Battle of Bunker Hill June 17.
Washington took command of the army July 2.
Boston evacuated March 17. 1776.
Independence declared by Congress July 4. 1776.
Hancock President.

Capture of Hessians at Trenton Dec: 26. 1776.
Capture of Hessians at Bennington Aug: 16. 1777.
Capture of British army at Saratoga Oct: 17.
Alliance with France Feb: 6. 1778.
Confederation of United States formed July 9.
Constitution of Massachusetts formed 1780.
Bowdoin President of Convention.
Capture of British army at York Oct: 19. 1781.
Preliminaries of Peace Nov: 30. 1782.
Definitive Treaty of Peace Sept: 10. 1783.
Federal Constitution formed Sept: 17. 1787.
and ratified by the United States 1787, to. 1790.
New Congress assembled at New York April 6. 1789.
Washington inaugurated President April 30.
Public debts funded Aug: 4. 1790.

· AMERICANS ·
WHILE · FROM · THIS · EMINENCE
SCENES · OF · LUXURIANT · FERTILITY
OF · FLOURISHING · COMMERCE
& · THE · ABODES · OF · SOCIAL · HAPPINESS
MEET · YOUR · VIEW
FORGET · NOT · THOSE
WHO · BY · THEIR · EXERTIONS
HAVE · SECURED · TO · YOU
THESE · BLESSINGS.

There may also be seen in this Hall a marble bust, on which is engraven the name of SAMUEL ADAMS. Of this noble patriot, who, with John Hancock, was by the British Government excepted from pardon in 1775, it cannot be amiss to say —

> " O, reader,
> Pass not on till thou hast blessed his memory:
> And never, never forget
> THAT REBELLION TO TYRANTS IS OBE-
> DIENCE TO GOD."

Samuel Adams and John Hancock were honored in one of the earliest songs of the Revolution, written by a British officer or soldier, in these words: —

> " As for their King, John Hancock,
> And Adams, if they're taken,
> Their heads for signs shall hang up high
> Upon that hill called Beacon."

Bronze statues of Daniel Webster and Horace Mann have been placed on the public grounds in front of the State House. The latter was dedicated July 4, 1865, with appropriate services and interesting addresses by Governor Andrew and others; that of Mr. Webster was inaugurated several years since, the late Hon. Edward Everett honoring his memory in an interesting and eloquent eulogy, in presence of a very large and attentive audience.

The rooms above are the Representatives' Hall in the centre, 55 feet square. Above the Speaker's chair are the Arms of Massachusetts, and Gilded Eagle, mentioned on page 11. In front of the Speaker's chair, suspended from the ceiling, on the opposite side of the Hall, is the Cod-fish which was first placed in the Old State House, in the year 1784, as appears by the following extract from the Journal of the House of Representatives : —

WEDNESDAY, March 17, 1784.

" MR. ROWE moved the House that leave might be given to hang up the representation of a COD FISH in the room where the House sit, as a memorial of the importance of the COD FISH-ERY to the welfare of this Commonwealth as had been usual formerly. The said motion being seconded, the question was put, and leave given for the purpose aforesaid."

In the east wing is the Senate Chamber, 55 feet long, 33 wide and 30 high, finished in the Ionic order. It is also ornamented with Ionic pilasters, and with the arms of the State, and of the United States, placed on opposite panels Here are preserved the portraits of several of the early governors of Massachusetts; namely, John Endicott, John Winthrop, John Leverett, Simon Bradstreet, William Burnet, Increase Sumner, and William Eustis, and of the Honorable Robert Rantoul.

On the wall in front of the President's desk are trophies from Bennington battle-field, and beneath them, in a gilt frame, the following : —

COMMONWEALTH OF MASSACHUSETTS.

BOSTON, December 5, 1777.

SIR, — The General Assembly of this State take the earliest opportunity to acknowledge the receipt of your acceptable present — the tokens of victory gained at the memorable battle of Bennington. The events of that day strongly mark the bravery of the men, who, unskilled in war, forced from their intrenchments a chosen number of veteran troops of boasted Britons ; as well as the address and valor of the General who directed their movements and led them on to conquest. This signal exploit opened the way to a rapid succession of advantages most important to America. These trophies shall be safely deposited in the archives of the State, and there remind posterity of the irresistible power of the GOD OF ARMIES, — and the honors due to the memory of the brave. Still attended with like successes may you long enjoy the rewards of your grateful country.

JEREMIAH POWELL, *President of the Council.*
Brigadier-General JOHN STARK.

The following is a copy of General Stark's letter to the Council : —

BENNINGTON, Septemr. 15th, 1777.

General STARKS

Begs leave to present to the State of the Massachusetts Bay, And pray their acceptance of the same, one Hessian Gun, & Bayonet, one Broad Sword, one Brass Barrell'd Drum, and one Granadiers Cap, Taken from the Enemy, in the Memorable Battle Fought at Maloonscott on the 16th of Aug't Last —

And requests, that, the Same may be kept in Commemoration of that Glorious Victory obtained over the Enemy on that day,

by the united Troops of that State, Those of New Hampshire,
and Vermount, which Victory ought to be kept in memory &
handed down to futurity as a lasting and Laudable Example for
the sons and Daughters of the Victors, in order, never to suffer
themselves to become the prey of those Mercenary Tyrants, and
British Sycophants, who are daily endeavoring to Ruin and
Destroy us — I am Gent : your friend & Humble Serv't

JOHN STARK.

To the Hon'ble Council
of the State of the Massachusetts Bay —

Near to these trophies are two fire-arms, the gift of the
late Rev. Theodore Parker to the Commonwealth. One
near the portrait of Governor Sumner, inscribed, —

" The First Fire Arm
Captured in the
War for Independence."

On the lock —

" GRICE
1762."

The other is placed above the portrait of Governor Bradstreet, bearing the following inscriptions : —

" This Firearm was used by
Capt. John Parker
In the Battle of Lexington
April 19th
1775."

On the lock —

" Theodore Parker 1850."

In the west wing is the Council Chamber, 27 feet square
and 20 high, with a flat ceiling; the walls are finished with
Corinthian pilasters, and panels of stucco.

The LIBRARY contains about 45,000 volumes; a copy of
Audubon's Birds of America; the laws of all the States in
the Union; several Historical Medals from the French Gov-
ernment; a portrait of Thomas Gage, the last of the Royal
Governors; and busts of George S. Boutwell, Rev. Arthur
B. Fuller and Henry Todd.

JOHN A. ANDREW,
War Governor of Massachusetts.

VIEWS FROM THE CUPOLA OF THE STATE HOUSE.

EAST WINDOW.

From this window are seen the Harbor, Islands, Wharves, and Shipping.

In front, on Somerset Street, is seen the meeting-house formerly occupied by the First Baptist Church, organized in the year 1665; the second centennial anniversary was celebrated June 7, 1865.

A little to the right, may be seen Faneuil Hall, termed "The Cradle of American Liberty."

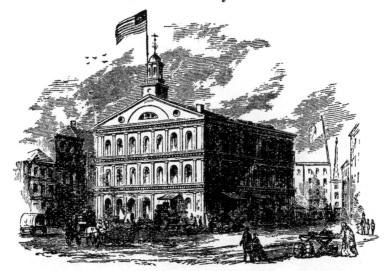

FANEUIL HALL.

Near to Faneuil Hall, is Faneuil Hall Market, the corner stone of which was laid April 27, A.D. 1825; it is nearly 600 feet in length, and 50 feet wide, and is situated between North and South Market Streets.

To the right of the Market, is seen the United States Custom House. It is in the form of a Greek cross, the

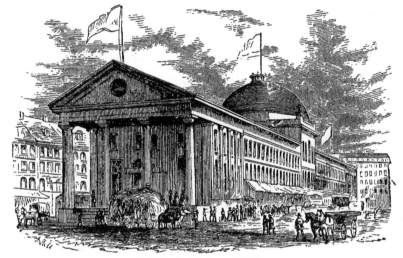

FANEUIL HALL MARKET.

opposite sides and ends being alike. It is 140 feet long, north and south, 75 feet wide at the ends, and 95 feet

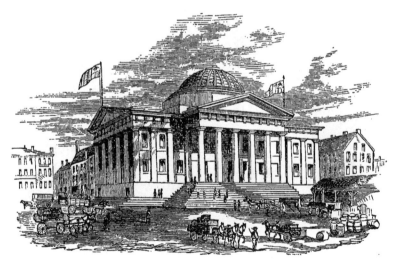

CUSTOM HOUSE.

through the centre, and is surmounted by a dome, which is 95 feet from the floor.

Nearly opposite the Custom House, is seen Pine Island. To the right of Pine Island is Governor's Island, and further n the same direction, is seen Fort Independence.

From this window is also seen the Old South Church, on the corner of Washington and Milk Streets, erected in

OLD SOUTH CHURCH.

he year 1730; in the Revolution profanely converted into a ding-school for Burgoyne's cavalry.

The Granary Burying-Ground, and the Horticultural Hall, ecently erected on Tremont Street, are also in sight, and cross the water is seen East Boston.

Christ Church, in Salem Street, built in the year 1722, is en from this window. Near to the State House, on Beacon treet, is seen the Boston Athenæum.

NORTH WINDOW.

The Reservoir near to the State House, is seen from this window. The basin holds 2,678,961 wine gallons of water.

ATHENÆUM.

To the right of the Reservoir, may be seen the Fitchburg Depot, on Causeway Street, near to which are the Depots of the Eastern and Lowell Railroads.

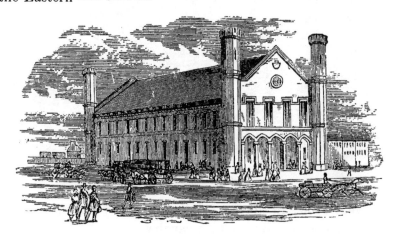

FITCHBURG DEPOT.

The tall chimney and round building to the right of the Fitchburg Depot, are the Gas Works. To the left, the building with trees in front is the Massachusetts General Hospital. The large brick building in front of the Hospital s the Medical College. The granite building to the left is he Suffolk County Jail.

From this window, are seen the Navy Yard and Bunker Hill Monument in Charlestown.

WEST WINDOW.

From this window may be seen many buildings lately erected on land formerly overflowed by the tide-waters, and known as the Back Bay. The Public Garden, several meeting-houses, — at the corner of Boylston and Dartmouth

HANCOCK HOUSE. Built, 1737; taken down, 1863.

Streets, the Old South. On the other side of Charles River s Brighton, to the left of which is Brookline.

The house of Governor Hancock could, until recently, be seen from this window; in 1863 it was taken down, and a magnificent structure of dwelling-houses has taken its place.

The following letter of Governor Hancock, transmitting a copy of the Declaration of Independence, is copied from the original in the Secretary's Department : —

[Massachusetts Archives, Vol. 195, page 73.]

PHILADA., July 6th, 1776.

HONDLE GENTLEMEN,

Altho it is not possible to foresee the consequences of Human Actions, yet it is nevertheless a Duty we owe ourselves and Posterity in all our public Counsels, to decide in the best Manner we are able, and to trust the Events to that Being, who Controuls both Causes and Events, so as to bring about his own Determinations.

Impressed with this sentiment, and at the same Time fully convinced, that our Affairs may take a more favorable Turn, the Congress have judged it necessary to dissolve all Connection between Great Britain and the American Colonies, and to declare them free and independent States; as you will perceive by the enclosed Declaration which I am directed by Congress to transmit to you, and to request you will have it proclaimed in your Colony in the Way you shall think most proper.

The important Consequences to the American States from this Declaration of Independence, considered as the Ground and Foundation of a future Government, will naturally suggest the Propriety of proclaiming it in such Manner, that the People may be universally informed of it.

I have the Honour to be

with great Respect

Gentlemen

your most obed't

& very hble serv't

Honble Assembly of Massachusetts Bay.

SOUTH WINDOW.

From this window is seen Park Street Meeting-House corner of Tremont and Park Streets; to the right of the church, on Tremont Street, is the United States Court House, formerly known as the Masonic Temple.

PARK STREET MEETING-HOUSE.

A little beyond Park Street Meeting-House, is seen the Music Hall. The Perkins Institution and Massachusetts

UNITED STATES COURT HOUSE.

Asylum for the Blind, on Mt. Washington, may be seen to the right of the steeple of Park Street Meeting-House.

In front of the State House is BOSTON COMMON. It "may be styled the great breathing apparatus of Boston. In summer or in winter those forty-eight acres of undulating ground, green with grass or white with snow, constitute a

PERKINS INSTITUTION.

favorite place of resort. And when the noble trees that abound there are thick with foliage, no more delightful promenade than those broad avenues beneath their interlacing boughs, could well be imagined."

BOSTON COMMON.